Species of Concern

SPECIES of CONCERN

poems by
AMELIA L. WILLIAMS

SHANTI ARTS PUBLISHING

BRUNSWICK, MAINE

SPECIES OF CONCERN

Published by Shanti Arts Publishing

Designed by Shanti Arts Designs

Cover image: pawel-czerwinski / dLp2YYJWoAI / unsplash.com

Shanti Arts LLC
193 Hillside Road
Brunswick, Maine 04011
shantiarts.com

Printed in the United States of America

ISBN: 978-1-962082-46-4 (softcover)

Library of Congress Control Number (LCCN): 2024950265

For my parents, and all the species of concern,
human and otherwise

CONTENTS

ACKNOWLEDGMENTS

Many thanks to the editors of the following journals in which these poems appeared, some in earlier versions:

American Journal of Nursing (AJN): "Flash Cards"

The Hollins Critic: "Walking the Celtic Ridgeway"

The Hopper: "Department of Agriculture Photographer, 1943"

JMRL/Writer House: "In the Field of the Ruined Piano"

Journal of Wild Culture: "The Cusp of the Known World: A Field Guide" and "Skin of Stars"

K'in Literary Journal: "Stay With Your Guide"

Nimrod International Journal: "Beautiful Death"; "The Catch"; "DIY Repairs"; "Inclusion Criteria"; "Overwintering"; and "We Say Stay Safe, Be Well—"

The Piedmont Virginian: "Red Clay Redoubt"

Poetry South: "Songs of the Red Velvet Ant"

Postscript Magazine: "Spiders Don't Say," and "Migrations"

Rabbit: "Idiosyncratic Attachments"

Shot Glass Journal: "Bio-Pic to Feature New Mega-Star, Hope"; "Charlottesville Anniversary"; and "Firefly Season"

Written Here: "At Mycenae Ruins"

"Gathering" and "Gowned in green tangle" appeared in the mixed media chapbook *Walking Wildwood Trail: Poems and Photographs*, 2016.

•

I acknowledge that I live in and write from the ancestral lands of the Monacan Nation, in the Middle James Buffalo watershed. I acknowledge all the efforts of the water protectors whose activism has inspired many of these poems.

•

Sincere gratitude to Christine Cote for the making of this book; to Cathryn Hankla for insightful reading and help with the big picture; for the care of your words to Mary Carroll Hackett, Debra Nystrom, Rita Dove, Sean Hill, Patricia Spears Jones, Brenda Hillman, John Most, and for incisive feedback to Nancy Allen, Basira Harpster, Hannah Loeb, Sigrid Mirabella, Molly O'Dell, Marian Pearce, Martha Snell, and Irene Wellman.

Thanks to the Hambidge Center, Palm Beach Poetry Festival, Breadloaf Environmental Writers, Nimrod Hall Writers, Tinker Mountain Writers, Community of Writers, Poet House, and Elk River Writers Workshop for time and space to write.

For standing with me, thanks to Max Johnson, Miles Johnson, Hanna Clark, Max R.. Much gratitude to Rollie Lawless, with love and thanks for countless hours wandering in nature looking at everything from lichens to flannel moth caterpillars.

"Now you feel how nothing clings to you;
your vast shell reaches into endless space . . . "

— Rainer Maria Rilke, "Buddha in Glory"

I

MY TRIP

I wake in a field of poppies feeling
a little hung-over, wearing red sparkly shoes
and a dress with an apron-thing, you know—
a pinafore. My familiar backpack is here,
phone has five bars. "Morning, are you all right?"

An art-in-the-park creature leans over me:
bicycle seat where a head should be, reflectors
for eyes, a crankshaft with pedals. In the chest
where Tin Man lacked a heart, I see gears
and a chain, well-oiled. "I'm Recycle," they say.

I give my name, though I'm not sure I'm still me.
"Is this a dream? I'm dressed like Judy Garland
in Oz and I may have bumped my head."
"Biped, I've seen stranger outfits than that.

We get these weird vortices—people fall through
all the time. I wish I were dreaming: my derailleur
and solenoid are both on the fritz—such luck!
So I'm off to see the wizard—you should come too.

She can schedule a transfer to your planet."
Oh great, it's not a dream. The shoes are pretty,
but not that comfortable. So I set off for Oz
with Peak Oil Sculpture, no Toto in sight.

The city is green all right. Wind turbines whirr
over small tidy gardens. Recycle says
they're organic. Roofs have solar panels
or sprout sod. Every being is made of wheels;
they move using the planet's magnetic fields.

How do they speak casual English, I wonder
but they say "No, it's the translational towers—
they let us understand one another's languages."
In the throne room the wizard offers me
latte and biscotti, and morphs from Oprah

to Mahatma Gandhi to a black cat playing
Tom Lehrer tunes at the piano. "Just tell me
where you'd like to go." When I say "Earth,"
onlookers spin their gears, flash lights, and mutter,
edging away. They put me on the first conveyance.

GONG IN THE MORNING

Oh gong in the morning,
who is coming to tap you
deftly in the clearing
among the cabins
along woodland paths

crackling with frost,
to reverberate your rim?
We mystics, penitents,

rising in the dark morning
in silence with toothpaste
and headlamps, hushed
before our spoons
of apple sauce, yogurt

from little containers
with noisy foil lids, yogis
of these disunited states

with white puffs of breath
gliding through the frozen
morning to the meditation
hall, aspiring bodhisattvas
here in the children's

summer camp cabins
waken to your golden
vibrations, taking turns

to ring and be rung,
golden bowl sounding
tender amplitudes,
call in the new year,
waken and call us in.

ON THE TAKE-YOUR-LIFE-IN-YOUR-HANDS
BATESVILLE ROAD

The nurse at 40 trains to cycle coast-to-coast—
a ride of self-discovery. Another idea drafts
and nudges ahead. A child, fatherhood, settle
down, maybe. He starts telling people,
"I'm going to get married," and when they ask,
admits, "I haven't met her yet."
                              The cheery,
big-shouldered doctor tugs their firstborn out
with forceps. She delivers the second swiftly
as his jacuzzi-dripping wife kneels on birthing
bed, vise-grips his hands, and bears down.
A few years later doc palpates the hard lump
in his belly and says in a measured tone they
haven't heard her use before and don't like,
"That is a little concerning. It is concerning."

SKIN OF STARS

Bring me onion skin, or vellum
        scraped with a lunarium for maps,
                transparencies, layers of almost
     knowing, linked patterns of transport,
                  arcane and common, drawn
       as branching vessels, a capillary
network, or dendrite-to-dendrite,
     inscribed on the land as song lines,
             fluvial and lacustrine landforms,
      as signs of glacier in arête and cirque,
        and in the sloped language of my home place,
its bluff and gully, knoll, defile, and draw.

For tonight I'm dreaming of the infant
     human skull with its fine sutures—
           coronal, sagittal, lamboidal—
    as if to follow the flyway home.
              I dowse for truths in patterns of
     marine migration, read the routes of
pelagic predators, tuck you in
     for the night with a lullaby of skins—
           fur, carapace, scales—and seeds—whorled
     pods of wingstem, the feathery
             tetrahedrons of goldenrod that
proudly persist through rain, wind, snow.

May I wake to continue dowsing
      as a tangle of filamentous fungi
            breaks down decaying matter
    to nourish soil, root, forest.
             With the ink of love, of cuttlefish alarm,
let us map our undercurrents, write
      deltas fed by distant rivers, mark
           springs bubbling up from doubt
    and fear, overlay the crab nebula
           on a sunflower seedhead, knowing
      we are one for all, running out, spilling
              over, flowing into and out of time.

SPIDERS DON'T SAY

I can't do this anymore   carry thread
          from leaf to laurel across   a vast deer-wide gap
                    each morning before   first light
only to have it broken   again

The spined *Micrathena* doesn't fret
          my babies will all get eaten   their slender silk streamers
                    lovely & light to carry them far   try not to be
          overbearing   maybe that's a mistake—if doing
my best doesn't change things for the better   what then

At home where the open & shut   of screen door
          tugs the spun funnel all summer long   *Tegenaria* repairs
                    its white skull-like foramina   elegantly angled
          for capture   beneath the porch light—
each slam vibrating a dangled detritus of mayflies & moths

Weaving a sheet web bowl to top a doily as elaborate
          as your grandmother's   not chiding the dew—
                    stop stippling my web to reveal what should remain
          cryptic—invisibility restored by mid-day—
the common *Frontinella*   lures a grass veneer moth to lunch

At a bend in the Rockfish I release your ashes
          near an almost-hand-sized striped fishing spider called
                    scriptus   w's on abdomen   this wily *Dolomedes*
          walks on water   bubble-dives to hunt—
gone fishing you would laugh   I gather a silvery orb of air

FLASH CARDS

Often we climbed Lookout Hill together to scan for hawks,
and sat on see-saw benches that skirt the fire circle. Our child
played happily stacking stones, singing times tables softly.

I gaze at the quiet ring where stone soup bubbled,
hear the scraping whoosh of a flash card
from my own childhood. My father, angry,

sent me back upstairs to try, try again.
Who can break the solitaire of shame
that shapes a child's fire for words?

The need for fast figuring still makes me tense;
brain blanks at casual arithmetic—to add a tip
my fingers move secretly, under the table.

Yet true crisis brought utter clarity—the pile-of-stones sound
as you dropped to the floor in agony triggered an orderly
checklist: wallet, diaper bag, baby, friend to watch toddler.

Cancer removed, your sternum-to-pubis surgical slash
was a colorful canyon of layers; the visiting nurse
taught me wet-to-dry wound dressing.

Four years later, the card I flashed, reluctantly,
was the emergency DNR, do not resuscitate.
The airport medic said I did the right thing.

I held your head so it wouldn't thump
as the ambulance rattled over potholed streets
in a distant city. Is he your father? they asked.

I talked to you out loud, in curtain number five
watched the subtle transubstantiation,
as two curves kiss, from living to living on.

LETTING GO: A FAIRY TALE

The red-faced skink scuttles away,
its blue and champagne stripes
flicker into a crack between boards.
A yellow smear on the side of the deck
reveals itself to be moving —
scores of pinhead-sized spider babies
flee their egg case.

The trail of bread crumbs
disappears; the hundred years' sleep
vanishes with a kiss; the sixth swan
wriggles its neck into a shirt of asters
lacking one sleeve, and is gone,
leaving a prince in its stead
with a wing at one shoulder.

I walk out of the neighborhood
and come to a crossroads. A wizened hag
basket in hand, remarks *bandits*,
pointing to the dusky woods. I give her
my arm. That's how it works; traveler
helps supplicant, endures frog's kiss,
removes a thorn from the wolf's paw.

Daughter, she advises, *don't dance*
with a spindle, or pin your cape
with the old tales. Pain's straw
can't be spun to gold, glass slippers
shatter; all you love may be cut short
as the braid of the maiden in the tower.

I nod my thanks. Have I done enough
to earn an elixir, a flint, ants' help? Midnight
tolls. Golden crab spiders long gone to yellow
roses, welcoming, open. Six white mice scuttle
away from a pumpkin—a carriage once—
its vast shell of grieving my only ride home.

STITCH ME

to this track, deer path, traced
by lichen, hoarfrost, common haircap, creeping cedar—
engraved threshold.

Last night's quarter inch of powder
and sun-tempered ice embroidered the woods.
I crunch over leaves.

Cliff trail my daily thread,
walking a rocking stitch
to hold my ground.

Granite and greenstone walls edge
sinking creek that trickles low
under roots.

Log where you used to sit—
sponge and crumble plastered
with pincushion moss.

At the bend, wild grape vines thick
as your wrist climb poplar thirty feet
for a spot in the sun.

Mountain laurel tunnel—
brittle, dark leaves curl under,
waiting for sap.

Hollow trunk where pilgrims stack
blue quartz, past the patch you showed me
springs ago, for chanterelles.

Home to faded pink-chimneys wedding quilt.
Red oak timbers, creaky in winter,
speak in your voice.

RED CLAY REDOUBT

We rinsed clay-tinged soap slurry from the floor
of the timber-frame house my husband was building.
The soil, just a quarter mile uphill

from the dark bottomland of the river
is red clay, dense, with an iridescent shine
where the shovel leaves its mark.

Digging footers we joked about our clay court.
It took two days of scrubbing with wire brushes
to release its hold on the dyed-cement floor

under the red oak timbers, mortised
with heavy chisels, graced with shouldered
dovetails, a mammoth ribcage ready for walls.

Pokeweed thrives in this stingy soil; I warn
the children not to eat the poisonous berries
as they finger paint with the luscious magenta juice

and daub lithe summer bodies before
tumbling and slipping in the inflatable
kiddie pool to rinse it all off.

Wild blackberry and bindweed love the clay,
and the tenacious herbs lay claim: thyme, mint,
oregano, lavender. When their father dies

we stay planted in soil once and again tinged with loss,
here in the foothills, the Blue Ridge rimming the sky,
among thoroughwort and lovegrass—pay dirt.

HOW TO WALK IN THE WOODS

Watch each footfall—track
    forest and sky. Periphery
        seethes. Note scent,
  sound, keep an eye out

and in. When root rocks ankle,
    seek soft dirt, not-quite
        mud. If saturated path
  shivers—find stable stone.

From trail to deer trace move
    swift as planning but before
        thought—drink in
hooded warbler's song.

Deep leaf pile may hide
    stumble hole surprise.
        Creek crossing's
  algae-green boulders,

dry last week,
    slick up in high water—
        so wade across; in froth
  toes grip tumbled rocks.

Small choices.
    Shoelace snags twig,
        heel smashes rotted log,
  pebbles roll,

scree sharp rattle scramble
    falter—hold. In tramp-trance
        step wide, stride over,
trek through, walk on.

GOWNED IN GREEN TANGLE

I trail cherry tomato vines'   explosive growth   to sprawl
out of garden bed   ramble across the lawn   climb the deer
fence   persist into late October   with globed red clusters
of six so sweet   to mash   against roof of mouth.

Years ago   your cancer receding briefly   I wound watchful
waiting around me   a pashmina scarf   like meditators use
warm ritual   hopeful as this black tortoiseshell kitten hovering
shy fosterling   not purring not cleaning its cobwebby whiskers.

After the cells mounted a new assault I assembled   other outfits
dressed in piling detritus   springing static-clinging   skirting
me magnetically   a not-quite-crinoline of dust bunnies   torn
calendar pages   unopened mail   crusty dishes.

Dressed for duty   opioid patches   gauze   remote control
bulging my pocketed vest   controlling remote   sensations
I bustled   competent movements   covering a caged dressmaker's
dummy   in crisp tailored Oxford cloth   prêt-à-porter.

In my closet is one I tried to give away   doesn't fit me anymore
but no one is falling for it   felted dress of   desolation over
leggings   leather-laced the way the conquered   Iceni wore
them   mud flat brown.

I travel now red-hooded   in hiking-boots   green corselet
falling away   past hemlock creek's stony riffle   to ridge of
beech trees I can't encircle   away from   or is it toward
the fangs   of the wolf that was my love.

GATHERING

We walk through the story at night
        whenever deer eyes cipher
                like fallen wind.
"Ky-ah?" my child asks, command
        to sing the word for a thing,
                wrinkling nose,
fierce fire to name worlds becomes
        my stone circle, strange gap for moonlight
                after river trickled ashes.
Eyes, fireflies, apples, naming—
        orchard-gathered sorrows, glowing road
                in red darkness, amid the fruit.

WANT WHAT YOU HAVE

In the woods there is so much movement:
    centipede sinuous
        ripple of synchronized legs,
            springtails bold,
unbraiding root, wooly bear marching.
      Wood frogs, quacking, erupt
        toward vernal pools—
  this hidden liveliness is called the sticks.
Sea urchin, hedgehog, stinging
        nettle—there are all kinds of spiky.
    We roll up around soft centers,
trundle into the world looking
    for something, assistant sustainability directors,
      gamma knife operators, resilience
award program managers, wondering
      who spiked the punch with wishes?

In the boondocks, almost at ease, notice
        powdered ruffle lichen,
     insect galleries of hieroglyphs under bark.
  Waxwings dip across
     creek's curve by the old sycamore,
  snails unretract glove-fingered tentacles,
       leave glistering trails.
    In nib, nub, hub, do they want
      what they have?
  Along twig of Chickasaw plum
    a saddleback caterpillar lights out
       at the speed of acceptance—
    from hither to yon.

II

STAY WITH YOUR GUIDE

1. Micro-Miniatures

At the Preservation Center our guide announces,
"In this top-security site, seed-material for our future
homes on other planets is thriving. Five of six
micro-biomes balanced after decades of effort.
The word *seed* will be explained during the tour.
Keep masks and gloves on at all times.
Despite the sensi-glass, we take precautions."

Colors I never imagined. Nothing real could be so pretty.
Everything moving—in the air, smaller than my pinkie nail,
things called birds, and bright-eyed four-leggers running:
horses. They said humans used to sit on their backs, and told
a story, fantasy I'm sure, how the creatures and green stuff
used to be huge, and alive on the surface. Just before
the Withering they shrank it all for safekeeping.

It can't be true. Gramma says
it's what they called bread and circuses,
flim-flam keeping us hopeful and obedient.
She heard her own Gram mumble about shrinks,
but thinks the old lady was confused, mourning
the past and dying of prions. Gramma says
they think we're stupid and will fall for anything.

2. Mood Studies Field Trip

"Class, gather 'round. Here is the sterile bench where we probe
sadness into bloom." I watch, transfixed—its ruffled, roseate petals
soften, fold away slowly to full open as if yearning

to tumble out, wilted but free. She stirs the shiny rod: "Often
we observe spectacular transformations." A rising flush
of burgundy-black creeps up from the center.

A ring of petals elongates to tentacles, reaches up,
and snaps the metal probe in half. The Lab Director
retracts her hands quickly,

"Though gloved, we move fast to avoid the piercing sting, a special
neurotoxin we call malevolin. It has stunning
properties." Sam looks right at me, mutters,

"Some people are stunned without it." Someone snickers.
"We're still trying to understand why the floral toxins
can be so potent." Our class on fungal and algal extracts

suggests choices: fusarium rot or adoration gel?
Toss-up. "Mice may exhibit jerky movements
and collapse. Others lunge at one another unpredictably.

No test subject has yet survived prolonged exposure to the petals'
kiss. Let's move on to euphoria. Studies suggest
that night-blooming jasmine may furnish some clues."

3. Inventor's Studio

Our guide is a cross between the Wizard of Oz
and Dr. Who. Excitement infuses his patter:
"These are some of our new witan!

The dancetron, morphogenulator,
rendarium. She's a real piece of work.
Step inside for the virtual demo. Anyone

heard of the old saunas? Our metaphysical
steam extraction memes your mind-body
somatithelium to a small vial of colored liquid.

No two vials are alike. Self-knowledge
is the key to success. We keep a drop
for science and return it to you."

I recite under my breath, "Render
unto Caesar the things that are Caesar's."
The guide pounces: "Indeed. You have a point.

Can you share that with the group?"
I shake my head no. He's trained to massage
sarcasm and smoothly continues:

"Our inventions invoke old adages, reminders
of a shared culture. It's about how you cope;
the process tells us more than we need to know."

MEDITATION RETREAT

The young woman beneath me coughed and coughed
all night in the cabin loft, the heat like scratchy
Easter clothes. I dozed at last into a treasure house

of my children's drawings, fluttering toward windows,
flying out into the street. You were there, love, a given,
a gift—trying to catch them.

What are thoughts falling through the mind
like snow? I always, should have, am not, can't ever—
let them go. Let them sip salts from the sandbar

like Clouded Sulphurs. I chanted: I have a little notebook
and I'm not afraid to use it. Bhante said everything
vibrates like electrons, impermanent.

I lie in the dark in this windswept cabin
and call you home. I am calling you to me.
I am calling on your kindred animals.

I need them to drink my tears.
May they be thirsty. O crow,
O bison. *Gate gate pāragate*

pārasamgate bodhi svāhā.
We have gone altogether, gone to the farther shore.
Fold me in that distance.

FIELD OF THE RUINED PIANO

"It's me or that piano." Their covered wagon groans to a halt
in a lush Appalachian meadow beside the buffalo trace
that widens up to the Cumberland Gap. Callous & loud,

no tenderness for what she loves: rosewood Chickering Grand—
all that's left since typhoid took her family; she wed in fear
of spinsterhood & hunger, wears regret like a muslin duster.

His gray wolfhound cowers whenever he speaks. "Unload it,"
she says, voice shaky, but brow determined, my foremother
Henrietta Schwab Funk, adding in imperious German,

"Now you may leave. I am staying to await the next wagon."
Her ochre-tinged cameo, in my red lacquer jewelry box
came with the gift of her story: she played for no one, only

meadow rue & crown vetch, a mournful nocturne, whose opening
notes fluttered like a mourning dove. All day, German dances;
that night she sheltered under the piano in her boiled wool cloak.

Sought a stream at dawn, found berries, chewed red clover, played
until fingers cramped & she grew afraid. Day five, listless, she lay
in the Chickering's shadow, aching with hunger, almost resigned.

Near dusk, the squeak of wheels. Tomas Guillaume, Acadian
fur trader, in an un-sprung cart, heading for La Louisiane.
Language no use to them, but his voice was kind, his tone amused.

No room for a piano. His gestures said they'd come back someday.
They shared bread & jerky, were wed with smiles & glances;
en route to the delta they traded words like pearls: *faucon, falke.*

A great love she bore him, the story goes, celebrated
especially in the field of the ruined piano; they'd return
in spring after selling the pelts. Soundboard cracked, keys warped,

music stranger each year, an off-kilter cascade echoing
Tom's bayou fiddle & stomp, Henrietta's labor cries,
the squeezebox of a girl whose great niece gave me the cameo.

DEPARTMENT OF AGRICULTURE
PHOTOGRAPHER, 1943

Fields of blue flax dance with bees, fuzzing
the August horizon. Old Joe Tipton
guides his Shire to mow. Nannie used to pull
flax by hand, yielding long fibers for cambric
and lace. Now we cut for linseed oil, cig
papers, banknotes. Lady photographer
from New York been following us all week.
Mostly silent.
             Finally shows us prints
from her field darkroom, talks a little—
long words like "fortitude." But her pictures
tell our lives all right: the Modlin sisters, Sallie
and Jessie, peer out from broad bonnets,
squint in the hard light, emptying a flatbed
trailer heaped with body-sized retted bundles
laid back into the fields to dry like rows
of graves.
             Me and Rachel Schoot in hot, heavy
filtration masks, feed the scutching machine,
grabbing straw to spread for combing.
Making pictures for a living—working woman
like me, but no children. She says, "maybe someday."
Now her USDA checks go to her mother's
TB sanatorium in the Ozarks. While we make
straw into gold for the government archives.

ATTIC LETTERS

Myrtle to Ed, October 3, 1952

Haywire is soft wire used to bind bales.
Breaks easily, goes all coiled and loopy—
so says the fat Brittanica—like gift
ribbon zipped between scissor blade
& thumb, or springy curls after
mother's hot iron & spray.

Something about how it got used
in penny-pinching New England
lumber camps, foiled their operations,
but honestly, Ed, I stopped reading
because the word *hay* got to me—I miss you
& home so much. Wishing for the scent
of the fall cutting or the sour whiff
of cow pies in the pasture. No chic
perfume; I'm a country girl I guess.

If we were rich we could talk
across the wires about the hay.
When I snuggle into your warm neck,
no cologne, but pine sap & sweat tell
the afternoon's story of splitting wood.
I'm going haywire here at the Normal
School where nothing feels it. Still,
I will keep at it & get good grades. Wear
your bandanna & mail it to me. Love, Myrtle.

Ed to Myrtle, October 15, 1952

Lyman brought the mail just as we started to pry
the old stalls from the barn. Like you say, nothing
feels normal. The horses miss your touch.
I walk into rooms still expecting to find you.

Write about your classes so I can show the letter
to your Ma; she'll love to see her old Remington
Porto-Rite still going strong. I know she'll tell me
again about ordering it from Sears Roebuck,
meeting the milk wagon to lug the thing home.

Remember, it's not her Oneonta Normal School now,
but State University College of Education. I brag
to the cows, "my wife is in college." Tomorrow we pour
concrete around the metal stalls. If it cures by Sunday
we'll plug in the new Surge Belly Milkers.

I enclose a strip of my bandanna around a sprig
of Houghton's Sedge from the bluff beyond
the gravel pit. Sketch it for your botany journal
and think of our last walk. 'Till November, Ed.

THE MEDICAL WRITER COMPOSES
ANOTHER DEATH NARRATIVE

Click through multiple spreadsheets, data tables, gather
the story the agency requires for each cancer patient
who dies during a clinical trial of an experimental drug.
Death narratives: demographics, disease characteristics,

medical history, prior surgery, prior chemo, diagnosis,
study regimen, serious adverse events, events leading to
discontinuation, procedures, labs, concomitant
medications, outcomes. Final disposition. Causality.

Write at least four a day. No personal information.

Demographics:
Subject #372, a 48-year-old
with a history of chronic diarrhea, considered
irritable bowel syndrome, was diagnosed with
ileal carcinoid cancer. Fine. But do not write:

History:
Subject joined a back-to-the-land commune at age 22;
became a woodworker, a psychiatric nurse. Played congas,
played the field. At 43 married a medical writer, designed and built
a passive-solar timber frame house, stayed home with their first.

Current Episode:
Ten o'clock at night clutches kitchen counter,
falls on the floor, all six foot four. Doctor says don't wait
for an ambulance. Neighbor says yes, I'll watch sleeping child.
Quick—pack up the diaper bag. Get subject and baby

into the car. In the passenger seat—moaning.
Never heard subject moan before. Fast, faster, bat out of hell,
cop lights flashing, pulled over—police escort to the ER.

Clinical Course of Events:
The subject presents with severe
pain and nausea and is NPO for three days. Abdominal x-ray
shows free air; exploratory surgery is indicated.
Before the gurney rolls through those doors: I love you.
Take my wedding ring. In recovery, subject groggily rouses,
asks what is it. Clutches her. Cancer she says. Fuzzes out
and back in, asks again and she says it louder: cancer.

The other patients and families stare.
The doctor names carcinoid cancer of the ileum,
between the large and small intestines. Excised.
What does it mean, cancer-like cancer? They learn together.
Scans show unresectable liver metastasis, no bone mets.

The subject's wife walks miles of corridor
jiggling the baby. Shifts of friends stay 24/7
so she can go home to the 4 year old.
Home health nurse demos wound

dressing changes for a fleshy gap of layered
pink and burnt-sienna like an aerial view
of the Grand Canyon. Neighbor holds infant.

Adverse Events:
The subject experiences
the adverse event of camping at the lake
with an ileostomy bag that keeps breaking loose.
Inability to rise from a toilet seat at a gas station.
The attendant lost the key—the cops break in.

Outcomes:
Times change. Now we write, *participants.*
The participant walks the loop road doggedly
'til strong enough for a second surgery to re-connect
bowels. Attends concomitant school picnics, first grade
soccer games. ECOG performance status 1; participant
returns to work on the psych unit. Neuroendocrine

cancer specialist moves. They fly to Albuquerque.
Octreoscan and petroglyphs. So much chili their stomachs
burn. A year later, drive to Tampa. Scintigraphy,

warm seas. Cuban food, pastel-colored cabañas.
Participant strolls through orange groves, bemused
that an "indolent" cancer has turned aggressive.

Treatments:
Ineligible for a clinical trial, participant undergoes
standard-of-care endocrine therapy with sandostatin,
(thousands of dollars per vial in the 'fridge, self-injected
daily) and fluoroacil, doxorubicin, cyclophosphamide,

erythropoietin, megace, vikoden, lasix, a fentanyl patch,
interferon alpha. Interferon is a bitch.

Follow-up:
Strolls down brick mall in the sunshine,
displaying bald head. They can't tell if I'm just cool
or if I have cancer! Humor that cuts close to the bone.
I can eat what I want. What's it going to do, give me cancer?

Before Cancer, had to be moving—tractor, volleyball court,
dance floor. Let's snap into action. After Cancer, wants forward
momentum and to feel warm again. No friends and neighbors
tiptoeing in with strained looks, hushed voices. A cruise: lemonade

on ship deck, Mayan temples. Pack up. Boxes of syringes.
Vials of drugs. Wheelchair. Children, lovies, and grandma.
Airport security looks in shoes, ignores the syringes.

Clinical Progression:
Poised for take-off on the tarmac in Philly,
Karl *with a K* dies due to heart failure, secondary to malignant
neoplasm progression. The medical writer puts the kids
in his lap. "Say goodbye." She wields the red-on-yellow
emergency DNR. Do Not Resuscitate.

AT MYCENAE RUINS

From brutal sun the dromos
plunges into a grassy hillside;
A girl of eleven years steps

into dark sudden chill
of the buried beehive dome.
She catches a scent, an essence

beyond motes of silt the tourists
kick up into a shaft of sun.
This royal tomb, the guidebook says,

held a gold diadem that signified
Agamemnon's storied bride.
Something hard—thin sandal sole

stubs a shard, red-glazed, faint
black spirals at the edge. Keen
fingers lift it swiftly to pocket.

Cup of Queen Clytemnestra
or modern rubble? Once home,
on city's edge where fig tree

and lavender hedge perch
above the Bosphorus,
she fashions it into a charm

with copper wire, leather strap—
wears it round her neck,
feeling fierce and feral.

All summer in pastures behind
the house she catches butterflies,
tracks tadpoles changing,

rules the tallest chestnut,
weaves nimbly in soccer
on cart-slicked cobbles.

In fall the amulet, clasped
in secret, parries ordinary
callousness of schoolmates.

Come winter, did it lurk
in pocket of attic clothes,
unrecalled in the next move?

No memory of when its
rough edge was no longer
a necessary talisman,

nor by what increments
eclipsed, that solid sense of
belonging to her whole body—

in womanhood's shadow
the glow of queen effaced—lost
too soon her best sharp knife.

HER VIEW OF THE CASTLE

battlements framed in bedroom window—
        zig-zag uphill to join stone towers

ripe fruit of hand-leaved fig near gatehouse—
        freedom to watch from sturdy branches

sulphur butterflies and fat tadpoles to catch—
        dismay at their fragility

dinner for foreign diplomats—by morning
        someone asleep under the piano

to meydan for süçuk sandwich—shopkeeper angry—
        Greek coins from her pocket dirty his counter

past crenulated tower, footpath around the dell—
        boy waiting to grab breasts she doesn't have

beyond lavender hedges, a hollow spot in the hazel bush—
        safety there, with notebook and pencil

burgundy wild cyclamen under horse-chestnut trees—
        a girl disappears into upswept petals

THE CATCH

Mending the net got this night vigil started,
   the fine green mesh thistle-torn from the chase
     for quick fritillaries in European fields.

My childhood collection's falling to dust
   in the attic, cotton wool yellowing, hand-inked
     labels brittle—Apollo, Common Brimstone—

butterfly bodies powdery with invisible bugs.
   Second prize in the science fair—puffed
     with knowledge: Latin names,

where to find egg clusters of Peacock and Painted Lady,
   how many drops of quick-acting poison
     from the entomological supply house.

The net gave this not-girly girl permission
   to speed through fields of weeds and brambles—the joy
     of a deft flick of the wrist to trap and hold

in careful hands the purple pulse of a Mourning Cloak,
   arriving faithfully each year as green spears and pale
     snowdrops nosed up through melting drifts.

One summer's home leave to Kansas I captured
   what I'd only seen in books—cousins of my familiars:
     Monarch, Buckeye, shiny sapphire rim spots

of Spicebush Swallowtail; still I longed to see
   the silk moth, Luna, whose leaf bud green
     ripples out into silvery tails, whispering

mystery and moonlight. I planned to wait by the garden lamp
in the warm summer night vibrating with crickets,
pierced with the vanishing hope of fireflies.

But my uncle, who'd been in Vietnam and come home
to raise tomatoes and corn, said I couldn't keep beauty
by killing it. I argued the cause

of collecting for science. But back in our gabled house
overlooking the Bosphorus, I put away the net,
pins, spreading board, sealed up the cases.

Now I'm sitting here in a pool of light
above fields of sumac in the Virginia dusk,
watching a bat flinging through the night

like a black serrated knife. Luna's flight
is languorous—weight set in motion,
the surprise of speed so graceful it seems slow—

she's night's creature, moon's darling,
you can't chase her through fields, but have to wait
for her to come to your beacon, light

a candle lantern, tuck fern leaf and violet
under your pillow, woo her gift of fertility,
listen for the whisper of wings beside the glow.

Years later, children in tow, hunting spring ephemerals,
by the seep, among the baby oaks, we see a lime-green
leaf move, fan newly-emerged wings.

III

EMBER DAYS

*Long ago, in the twenty-first century, linguists had time
to dispute the origins of the word ember—ymbren in the
ritual called Ymbren Dagas.*

Let us gather at nearest dry fountain,
cracked pool, trickle, puddle, thin creek,
trough, salted sea, to weep. We draw tears
on our cheeks to signify. Thanks be for
all waters that may yet return to us as rain.

Yearly we join hands to honor our named giants—
ten monument trees—or a hallowed cultivar
tender in unbreakable arborium, or (guessing
it's true there are a secret well-guarded few)
a wild copse whose breathing gives us breath.

Come parade around our racks of pot herbs,
rooftop gardens, raised beds, hoophouses,
fields of guild-tended crops; march,
dance, sashay—teach the young what harvest
used to mean and sing—beat the bounds.

Hum, buzz, intone, vamp a sound for
all six-legged who yet remain to carry
pollen, praise each yellow grain and raise
your horse-hair pollinating brush, grateful
whenever you have no need of its fine point.

IDIOSYNCRATIC ATTACHMENTS

1. Saving Jack Mountain

A summer storm gathers on the shoulders of Jack Mountain.
Drops patter on scree. Timber rattler eases off
warm greenstone and riven shale,

slides to wait out the downpour in her dry communal den.
In the draw below ascending ridges of old-growth trees,
springs trickle down through a sea of wood nettle,

its tiny sprays of seed-pearl blooms an afterthought
in a spill of green. Thick chestnut oak and hickory shelter
ebony spleenwort, bearcorn.

We walk up the winding trail, noon quiet but for Linne's cicada,
through abundant motherwort, elderberry,
crownbeard, and curly dock.

Cerulean warbler buzz-trills in dampened heat. I try to imagine
the entire teeming ridge flattened, scraped, hauled away in
400-ton-payload trucks the size of two-story houses.

Pearl crescents alight and sip on fallen fruit. Tomorrow
I'll return to the work of resistance. I reach through thorns
today, gather wild raspberries, and eat.

2. Floaters

In the chair at the eye doctor
dilation drops begin to take effect
my edges waver

                          crossed loosening
                            braid sinuously
                                 opens

physicists say matter
is mostly space

                            is mostly space
                   a floater like an untwisted
                            skein of yarn

squashed harvestman
or cranefly with dangling legs
appeared in my right eye

                           as I leaned over
                     the glass wind chime
                 twisting copper wire around

small mammal vertebrae—
arches of bone make
protective spaces

                     for the spinal cord—
                 braided like the carpet
              I sprawled on, working pliers

coiling wire to jam
into the bottle neck of green-tinted
bell-strung mobile, rope

                         thrown over
               high hickory limb above
                  mirroring cistern

prayer beads arrowhead honey jar
bones and stones clinking
when wind blows

                  through all the trees
              they would cut down to build
          their damned fracked-gas pipeline

floater unnerving
like mitochondria and gut flora teeming
inside warning against imagining ourselves
more substantial than not

3. *The Stone Tribe*

Drawn to them—glinting, grooved or pocked,
water-smoothed, immutable, dull pebbles,
till spit-rubbed, true colors unlocked,
we bulge our pockets, stucco shards
to chimneys, fill jars and trays.

Beyond geology we know their power—
at scree slope or cave mouth we gather
rocks as runes, build signal cairns,
seek geode secrets, mountain bones.
Earth's crust once pleated in orogeny

like bridal organza. I palm this keeper
from a Cowpasture River sandbar,
oval brown, with a creamy, pinpricked
band, like smoothed coral, a talisman
for these rough days of fracture.

4. Entwined

Braid our ties that bind, our scraps, strands
             wrapped around their kin. Fluffed
                     knit scarf clasps damask green
of an old curtain, Oma's flax shirt.
                   Here a blue spine, open, admits
                           rivulet, rill, flumes of air, jaunty
                               pinnatifid bows where we add on
                    a new strip of silk. Flounces
commune with shiny sleeves,
                  unchained persistence hums
through the threads, twirled
         like fox grape and greenbrier
             climbing toward light. We
are tied to these mountains,
          rooted by choice where the black
               snake may slither, fracked-gas threat named
                     by elders who have seen it all
              before—dark petrochemical trail.
Watch our colorful braided coil
           unhinge its jaw, swallow.

"IN YOUR DREAMS LUNA IS GREEN"

the voice insists,
>   but I haven't been dozing. I notice the porch light is on.
>   Then there's a face at the door.

> *I know it's late. He was just in the kitchen, with a knife,*
> *and he was upset, so I got scared and came over. I hope it's OK.*

Of course. Come in. Moth flutters somewhere between
>   the color of cucumber magnolia pods
>   and a not-quite-ripe Anjou pear.

> *He said he hadn't been sleeping while I was away.*
> *He wasn't sure if he'd taken the anxiety pills or the sleeping pills.*

In your dreams, *Actias luna*—not my anxious voice. Of course,
>   I think, it's green. Beats wings against the small sun, dazed,
>   losing powdery scales. I'll make lavender-mint tea.

> *The pill minder wasn't the right shape, he said,*
> *so they didn't all fit into the right day, and he lost track.*

Exigency, pheromones, mouth that cannot feed, all it entails—
>   verdant wish for refuge, hopes pin you, spotlight burning,
>   on the spreading board of the ethereal feminine.

> *I just left in my housecoat and slippers, not thinking*
> *how unseasonably cold it is, this September.*

TWAYBLADE

In May the lily-leaved twayblade
sends up   inconspicuous
          green and mauve-washed blooms.
          It is a species of concern in parts of its range

and below the logging road where neighbors want
to build.   To write about
          the woods is also to write
          about the fracked-gas compressor station

slated for Union Hill community,
descendants of formerly   enslaved.
          The historian says the Monacan kept trying
          to move farther away from thieving

deadly Scotch-Irish, my volatile ancestors,
who survived   brutal Norman conquest.
          On the ridge above our lily-leaved ravine
          neighbors dream more houses. Twayblade in May—
an almost imperceptible species of concern

in some variegated parts of its range.
Free from gas blowdown's   volatile
          organic compounds one county over,
          we craft actions, letters, hopes scandent
as crossvine in fracked slate counties.

Stolen, says the Monacan historian,
*from my ancestors;   all of the woods
          and creeks I love kept trying to move.
          Away, murderous settlers, farther.*

Landowners fight Dominion the papers say,
without irony,   about the unceded woods
    I love, unsettled   by wild orchid seeds
    that depend on fungal rhizomes. May

woods write their love notes unfrac-
tured by threat of   thieving, dire
    formalities,   cherishing irregular
    blooms that dangle

BAKED ALASKA

Frozen pound cake and   our warming climate is having
two pints of the best vanilla   serious, broad-scale impacts:
ice cream, 6 large egg whites   permafrost thawing, villages flooding
fresh lemon juice and sugar   eroding coastal beaches,
slice the frozen cake to   subsidence—when heavy structures
line the pan entirely   sink deep into the ground

Cut ice cream into rounds and   we have six types in
wedges, filling holes to   the greenhouse gas inventory:
cover the cake completely;   carbon dioxide, methane, nitrous oxide
place it in the freezer. Pre-   perfluorocarbons, hydrofluoro-
heat the oven to 450°   carbons, and sulphur hexafluoride.

Beat egg whites and   Alaska's gross greenhouse gas
a pinch of salt   emissions grew at a faster rate than those
with an electric mixer   of the nation as a whole;
until foamy, then add   the principle source is
lemon juice, continuing   industry, followed by transportation,
to beat until whites   industrial emissions
hold soft peaks; gradually   from coal mining, oil, and natural
add sugar, beating until   gas production, processing,
peaks become stiff and glossy   transmission, flaring,

Mound the meringue over   fugitive methane,
the frozen base. Bake   oil refining;
in the middle of the oven   mitigation options
until golden   recommended in this report
brown about six minutes: are not sufficient
serve immediately   to reach our goals.

DEAR HUMAN

I'm not sorry. Sweat-dampened
red cloth blossom—your hat resting on ground
while you ate lunch—my landing pad.

You didn't notice me? Exactly. Black, nickel-sized
bee or wasp, you aren't sure? Call yourself
an amateur naturalist? Show me some love.

Your "put my ball cap back on" is my "tried to crush me
against its big head," so I stung. You're outraged.
Your eye swelled shut. For days.

When your teacher handed out range maps of birds
you got the green heron and wished it would eat me.
But your map says nope. Not since the seas withdrew

in the early Cenozoic were there swamp bird ancestors
in Montana. All the same, I'd rather be eaten
by a snake-necked marsh-loving avian

once widespread from Colombia to Florida,
and Baja up to the redwoods, than be smashed
when you don your hat. Sad to say our

iridescent green and wine-throated fisher is in steep
decline. Come to think of it, my kind are suffering too.
Unapologetically Yours, Four-Toothed Mason Wasp.

IV

GETTING CLOSER

These fluted, feathery shafts are an insect's
compound eye, enlarged. Fimbrae of fallopian
tube flutter rose-petaled across the next page.
After this elegance, the tardigrade.

Magnified merely two hundred and seventy
times, it looks like a challah with plump hands—
almost cuddly. *Tardus*, slow-moving water bears
or moss piglets, the largest species big as

poppy seeds, but most requiring a basic
microscope, eight-legged shar-pei-folded
doughboys, survive extreme temperatures,
radiation, boiling, the vacuum of space.

Fine-focused to times three thousand, cute
evolves an alien maw ringed with spikes,
waiting to devour. Granted their own phylum,
like chordates in the mnemonic, they play chess

on fine green silk. Unaware of the dismissive
schoolyard taunt, "Oh dry up and blow away,"
they tuck in legs, roll into an obliging ball:
cryptobiosis. Meeting moisture they revive.
Guess who's going to inherit the earth?

MEDITATION WITH THE SIEVE ANGEL

Delirious with headlines,
I wake from an anvil dream;
blood hammers my temples —
disaster, privation, shards fall.

Be blacksmith and open mesh,
at one with flake and flurry.
Temper anger with compassion.
What? Who's there? *Sieve Angel,*
spun silver in Gramma's snow globe.

Her filigree-skirted angel sat quiet
on the mantel for years. The air
grows chill; I shake my head; snow
swirls up, wind plays through me.

A loving kindness meditation:
let's begin. When thoughts interrupt,
notice, and continue breathing;
they pass, like wind-carried snow.
May I be kind, (thinking: one of a kind

two of a kind, kindred), gentle
in speech, smooth as riverstones.
May my teachers, seen and unseen,
be free from fixed views. (I want

an avenging angel, sieve Shiva.)
May the ones I love be free
from suffering. (Who can seek justice
without anger?) *Breathe in darkness,*
send out light; taking in and giving

away—these two shall ride the breath.
Snow settles, stills. Invert it again. May enemies
within and without be safe from harm.
Can you see your breath in here?

SASSAFRAS ECSTATIC

When I hike in the mountains I like to take a twig
of sassafras and scratch the bark. Its warm candy-shop
clove and allspice scent cheers me over the steep hills.

In the '60's word came down from the FDA—
Gramma's sassafras tea, and the root beer we drank
with extracts of sassafras and sarsaparilla,
kicking our heels in the August dust on the porch
of Greenfields Market, gave liver cancer to mice.

They banned sassafras oil from the root, and later
the soothing tea, but allowed us filé for gumbo
from the one-finger, two-finger, three-finger leaves.

Safrole, to blame for all this mess, also skulks
in cinnamon and nutmeg, and on the HERP Index
(Human Exposure/Rodent Potency), is sandwiched
between lettuce (caffeic acid) and orange juice
(d-limonene) as a possible human carcinogen.

Banned in the 80's, distilled from Asian safrole,
it would take a whole forest of Appalachian
sassafras roots to extract a few doses of X.

A tiny armored vehicle, the redbay ambrosia
beetle, threatens what backroom molly makers
couldn't: to destroy our native sassafras. It carries
laurel wilt fungus in mouth pouches to new terrain,
plants and harvests a crop of fungal sweetmeats.

Not scoffing to brew sassafras tea, this vaxxing
helmet-wearer challenges her liver with wine, 3.6
on the index to safrole's 0.03, insouciant and spicy.

INCLUSION CRITERIA

You put in the photo of the young man, Oscar, face down
in the water. A kid nearly, only twenty-five, and Valeria, his child,
drowned in the Rio Grande trying to make it across
from Mexico to the US.

He's the same age as your oldest; his child could be your grand-
daughter. You put in *Aren't we all part of the same human family*,
then cross it out. Her red leggings are luminous. Sharpened focus,
in the foreground, grass reaches tapered blades

across the river's pearly sheen, touching them both,
wrapped together in his wet t-shirt, above a buffer of river cane,
littered with bright blue beer cans,
one shucked rubber glove.

You leave out the swollen rush of the nearby creek,
the butterscotch smell of Jeffrey pine, fox sparrow's
insistent song. Dry-eyed, you pencil tears down the side
of the page. It is not possible to go on putting things in.

MIGRATIONS

We could have learned from the cinnamon tufts
of sulphur firedot, or dark outlines
of yellow map lichen, their fungal, algal,
and yeast layers deftly feeding one another,

and from mitochondria—that ancient
migrant caravan; they made it across
our border. Now enclosed within our
semi-permeable membranes, they keep us

alive. Cooking up our energy, housed
in the cells we shape for their shelter—
are they us, are we them? They build us.
Inside our bodies we are munificent,
adaptable, prone to self-replicating
networks of fractal beauty, diasporic joy.

CHARLOTTESVILLE ANNIVERSARY

August 12, 2018

Dark torrents of rain make mist on the mountains
swirl like cobwebs I catch with my broom.
August air's thick—a damp woolen passage
for muck that oozed from soil near my home.

Mars has come close, its blood-orange gleam
hangs three fists up in a darkening sky. Mold
blooms on leather chairs, silverfish scuttle,
a Hebrew moth comes to my outside light—

its black loops on white a powdery sigh.
Along this dirt road past the old country store,
roots of the hanging-tree, scar tissue exhumed—
of all that's exposed, what part is mine?

TO AN OVEN BIRD WHILE
SHELTERING IN PLACE

White spotted breast, orange and black
on your head—I wouldn't have seen if you
were not warm in my hand, but dead.

I nestled you in woods-edge laurel,
fetched the soap for crosshatch bars
to mark south-facing windows.

In this rural calm, so far spared
the siren's wail of despair, we wait,
worry, wash hands, wear masks.

Unable to see our path, in tangential
grief, make stark the barrier we built—
a warning, I hope, this tic tac toe of soap.

OVERWINTERING

This season of hunkering down distanced, masked,
I walk for relief along the creek, over muddy runnels
where a spring crosses the path,

and bushwhack up a steep ravine, crunching through the palette
of leathery browns I have come to love: chestnut oak, poplar,
hickory. I know how to go here, where I could slip,

to grip a sapling, testing first, lean against a fat trunk,
rest burning calves. A word, *unceded*, rattles
like a beech nut in its shell, prickly as sweet gum

seed pods that resemble a virus. I notice a pale green scrap
you could mistake for desiccated corn husk, perhaps,
or a wind-blown shred of grandfather's puckered

seersucker beach-and-umbrella-drinks shirt,
strewn sere, elliptical, over late-season litter—
puttyroot orchid's papery wisp.

They wait till unencumbered branches clack
to put forth a single leaf, bask in thin winter sun,
gathering strength required to retreat.

Come June they send up a single stalk
of insect-shaped flowers, each purple-tipped part,
from yellow-green sepals to frilled

white clamshell lips, so delicately lovely
you'd become a bee just to get inside.
How are you holding up, we ask,

the news a Möbius strip of our past. Orchid
feeds its unseen tuber that settlers were taught
makes putty to mend broken pots.

WE SAY STAY SAFE, BE WELL—

these are the middle layers of the artichoke—
but I'm getting ahead of myself. First trim
the thick stem, remove tough
protective bracts. Cut angriest tips
from layers that clutch, not thorny, but prickly
like me, tense with fear and recycled news:
deadly force, respiratory distress.
It's a thistle, after all, well-defended.
Dip in lemon butter, steam 'til edges relax,
pull away, leaf by supposed leaf; don't they
taste faintly of nuts? Reach inner rings,
translucent petals, cynarin's flavor almost
cloying, cut tender heart into pieces, eat.

BEAUTIFUL DEATH

Cave mouth dark, tunnel darker still;
only my headlamp saves me from the left fork
that would break my leg.

Walls give up secrets. Heralds with geometric
burgundy, amber, and ochre marks, and paler
lacy tissue moths, glitters of purple.

Air shifts, walls gleam with drops. Going deeper,
I find what I have come for: white
flowering out of the back wall

like blanched coral miniatures, snowflake
cutouts shrunk to faerie size:
clusters of moths, beautiful

death growing from their bodies: *Cordyceps* fungus,
whose long white fingers reach out
to exude spores into perfect cool humidity.

Days later my friend turns away from my photograph,
distressed for the moths. Only then I feel sorrow
for what I made lovely, forgetting to mourn.

SONGS OF THE RED VELVET ANT

1. *Soliloquy*

O honey bees, true ants, and paper wasps—
my social cousins who know the nectar dance,
lay trails of scent for comrades, construct
elegant paper houses, how I envied
your winged chance to savor pollen, tousle
blossoms, touch antennae—to belong.

When my mate carried me up in nuptial flight
it wasn't my dreamed-of bliss, no honeyed song.
Now I strut along in my red velvet dress,
drawn like daggers to the mouth of a nest
in my finery. Emitting foul perfume,
stridulating at the least threat, I can't help but
lay my eggs in the ground bees' open brood cells;
my children are destined to eat theirs one by one.

2. Cow Killer, My Eye

I'm shy in truth, but you in your sandaled feet,
naked toes, step aside fast to notice me
strutting down the dusty path. Floozy,
you're thinking, sashaying around in that red
velvet dress. Yeah your friend gave you shit
for anthropomorphizing me. But sugar—

I'm imagining you too. Some nights
in a dream of flight we explore the heart
of a foxglove together, sip and suck,
slip pollen from anther in a speckled cup.
Awake, both back in our armor, no signals
to send. I've wrapped you in my story.
Implacable, you enter the nest of the other
to lay your eggs. Do we belong together?

DIY REPAIRS

What we need in our kit
is a sticky probe—
duct tape you can roll
inside out around a chopstick, say,
to fish things out
of places dark & narrow.

My brother's hernia was patched
with animal webbing he reabsorbed.
He hasn't visited Mom in four years. As if
her plaques & tangles were contagious.

I've scraped the undersides of bark
for tinder. Now spark, dammit, spark.

I dowse. I fine tooth comb.
I chanterelle & dollop.
I palette knife, all thick & wavy.
If mending a rift could be
like wild-gathering: blackberry,
daylily, morel—no measure, no sift.

It's a press fit means
pound it into place.
It ain't a church, because
only you will notice a sixteenth
of an inch or the chipout
we fixed with CA glue.

We mesh all together—
grandbabies, nieces, stepfathers,
children of the gas station clerk,
cousin of the boy I took to prom,
& the stylist from the salon,

you know the one—
stepdad had the DUI,
kid got picked for Berklee.

Maybe the thermocouple is still OK;
turn on the pilot, give it a click.

How love's pliers grip the bolt
while one of us strips the threads.

BARK EMBROIDERY

after Diana Yevtukh

Under the bark of the poem
run embroidery threads.

What a decorative way to sew
something shut.

Behind the stitchery, phloem,
cambium, & sapwood nourish

& grow; in hollows made by one kind
of damage or another, granivores

hide seeds, sow them in the crannies.
In the nooks of this poem or that,

we huddle together to learn
about snakes & kleptothermy.

Tonight, speak no sorrow—instead
fetch me a needle & colorful thread.

V

NEW MEGA-STAR

A rainbow shimmer—found cowering in a corner
of Pandora's box. Hope. "Great wings," they said,
"but the look too ingénue." The bioengineers are on it:
"We can re-make you; silnylon and aerogel here,
titanium there." Marketing is testing *avenge*,
virago, and *harpy*, in titles with an upbeat spin.
The ills and evils have long since flown off,
or lumbered away. Hope's new publicist, Glory,
tells us, "She hasn't hit her stride yet; ethereal,
yet charismatic—not your typical starlet. Hope
has devoted fans. Call her a serious dreamer."

SPRING MORNING MEDITATION

Through half-closed lids, a meadow seeps:
deadnettle's lavender flowers, fleabane petals
tinged pink sharpen under lashes, then blur,
a wash of lime persimmon crossed by twigs.
Make note of tears.
                              Birdsong trickles in.
Struggle to let it go without naming, fail
until chick burr confirms scarlet tanager.
A bee homes in on campion; the sound
stops briefly, then the soft buzz rides off;
there's a faint gobble of wild turkey in the woods,
and my neighbor's rooster beyond calls *alive, alive.*
In the mix I hear, not as bold as the Carolina wren,
nor subtle as the worm-eating warbler, the phrases:
honeycomb interstitial infiltrates, tree-in-bud nodules,
and *ground glass opacities.*
                              The future is opaque;
now the breeze is on my skin, now the wood thrush
sings melodic double-notes into the air around us,
all atoms of all breaths. On the outbreath I clench,
not unstinting—not wanting to give it all away.

ANEMONE TALKS BACK

Alright, I lay there for a while, pale, tired—
can you blame me? Maybe I did accessorize
with fear—explore the hinterlands.

The forest wild was heavenly at first. I was devoted.
Ephemeral petals dropped, water bubbled like a spa.
No family, colleagues, tabloids, BFFs.

It's not that tangled, really. I loosened myself
from shadows, vibrating like the lesser
anglewing playing solo in the bushes.

This flourish of shiny leaves—my crown of refusal.
Took a new word, broke up with the old—
fortune, femininity, faint praise, frog prince, all

the old inheritances, those f-ing assumptions.
Exhorted to buck up, look lively, give us a smile sweetheart,
I put a stop to it. They say I fanned the flames.

Can't let slip. That would be telling. Now I'm restless,
following a faint trail through tough ruddy branches
in the laurel hell—hands and knees, no easy

day hike. Evanescent deer-forged tracks lined with parachute
Kalmia, bony-fingered now, when closed,
but soon mouths open, stippled with red—

that's first blood, princess, be proud. It's no one's fairytale,
with handoff to a new animal guide—spicebush
swallowtail leading; my band of gold stretches

wide and unafraid on either side of the raging river.
Fringe of yellow blooms marries woods to water—
wild redoubt for the queen's daughter.

MAKING TIME

"... the universe is creating not only new space, but also new time."
Richard Muller, NPR, September 27, 2016

My high beams rake the distance, catch
the dead on the side of the road: the raccoon
enters this space, recasts a simple drive home.

The hazelnut hedgerow was nearly hollow
between the greenery and trunk. At twelve,
I could just fit with a rug, stool, and notebook.

The waxing gibbous moon shines through
the windshield; above the winter trees
Orion tilts rakishly. What moment is this?

Time was fluted maroon cyclamen,
the sound of ferry horns floating uphill,
scratch of colored pencils on heavy paper.

Time to pull over and get out. Moon glow
throws shadows of fence posts, cedars;
eyes are shining under the apple trees.

In the woods where I first conceived
of our love, I sometimes sit and ring myself
with golden leaves. This makes a new time

to make new space, in windswept broom moss
near the cliffs, skin to skin in our little bed under
the stairs, a kitchen in the cave of dawn.

I OPENED FOR YOU

faint and misty like the ridgeline you see from Orchard Hill
each morning, scented with something you can't name but nearly
taste—cardamom, cumin?
                            Bardo. You heard Rinpoche. After you
lighten your pack, eat the sardines and palak paneer,
a first-night supper of heavy items,
                                    between the moment stars pop
in the dark sky and the harvest moon rises, rimmed ochre
this October night that threatens frost.
                                    Fissure, rift, breach, hiatus.
We coil tight in down bags on a high overlook
one ascent past Cole Mountain.
                            Inside the gap I tattoo
forgiveness, flay you with feathery touch, cheek
against your warm chest, grip shoulders
                                    in a hug so tight
it might be an evasion. Luminous gap. Not unlike Reed's Gap
at 7:52 PM in the last steps of cautious descent,
                                    as sun flares
briefly, then dips, erasing the glow on all leaves—rust, yellow,
salmon—to hide loose stone cause a near-misstep.
                                    Afraid
in the dark we arrive in the saddle of the gap. Ambulance
lights attend a crash. Each strobe shows
                                    cells and fluid,
shifting handful of onlookers, mere tissue, pulsar
dependencies; overhead, above Markab and Algenib,
al-Sufi's great horse.

I FELL IN LOVE WITH MOUNTAIN GAPS

In the west they say pass   not for dying I mean
but instead of gap   like we say back east

Reeds Gap   Rockfish Gap   Jarmans Gap
wind gaps formed   by stream capture   as waters

leave   their original bed   diverted from initial
flow-current-coulee   lively creek   abandoned

for the valley of the shadow   left me in the spark gap
the space between   two high-potential   terminals

often filled   with an ionizing gas   a pass has several
options   defile   saddle   col   should I close

fill   breach   dearth   years after you died   I made
a pass   on a knoll enticed him   from South Anna Valley

WALKING THE CELTIC RIDGEWAY

where generations
>   have trod through Wiltshire odd to step
>   poppies blowsy in breeze
white chalk horses
>   grassy tumuli

>   another trail runs beside my actual life
>   ambition's ghostly apparatus
>   I can almost make out a figure
>   through the mist running
>   she turns
>   to jog backwards for more challenge
did I fail to take that path

>   or choose not to
my way like Spirograph cogs
>   around cogs of job house children
>   holding hands on pebble paths until surprise
>   a flower a snowflake the bloom of cancer
>   loop-de-loop my husband's tilt-awhirl surgery
>   scintigraphy
>   chemo
>   death

>   my tears on the blue mat during savasana
in-breath
>   trailing out-breath
>   water a plan
>   to follow the Celtic road
>   called the Ridgeway
>   the track we now tramp
>   sheep's wool
>   gathered in bramble thickets
>   shining downy dusk

with my young sons and new lover I circle
    the Avebury stones
            pass strange seekers pressed reverently
against the warm granite
                climb grassy hill forts where markets used to be
            into the dark mouths
                        of long barrows we peer
                    getting on the way people do not
                                    saying
                        what they love enough

THE CUSP OF THE KNOWN WORLD:
A FIELD GUIDE

October mornings we wake to raspy buzz and jingle—
the Lesser Anglewing's salsa shaker egg, Two-Spotted
Tree Cricket, smoke-detector loud, and sweet chirp

of Allard's Ground Cricket—or is it? We press "play"
again to hear a competing candidate for this trilling,
pronounced in a clear Midwestern voice: Say's Trig,

he intones, *Anaxipha exigua.* When efforts to distinguish
overwhelm, we relish our insect musician names:
the Slightly Musical Conehead, the Dog-day Cicada.

> *I feel we are on the verge of something. A marriage*
> *between cup and clasp. Two curves lean*
> *into one another, stretch upward with cautious*
> *yearning, as if on tenterhooks, waiting,*
> *just hung out to dry, the wet woolen smell*
> *on the edge between musky and rank.*

The field guides agree it is hard to pin down
a goldenrod. We sort them into tribes by shape:

plume-like, club-like, wand-like, and elm-branched.
It can be hard to tell a wand from a club. Don't forget

the flat-topped clusters. Asters, likewise, are tricky.
Leaves give clues: whorled, crooked, toothed or not,

grass-like or perfoliate. In astonishing profusion
the tiny white asters are almost unknowable.

What are we on the brink of here?
It could just be me, stridulating,
hatching out of my skin of knowing, naming,
claiming; empty of easy kinship. Fall is
alive with the strangeness of yellow
flower, red berry, swift dark flying,
rattling upriver, not toeing the line
but towing it, pulling up stakes,
uncinching the taxonomy of love.

DARK CANYON

we hike this slot   canyon trail—shallow
waters bubble along   movement all that matters
sorrow unwinds to slaking   I remain open to passages
              there might be a cave

or curtain stalactite   in a wet lunge the river could rise
possibly the breath   taste in your kiss surprise of red
penstemon billows   now pebbles slip hurry
              like liquor a heady feeling

when I am split   in your arms in muscles
out of one place into   another smooth concentric
cling wrap not your usual   sedimentary slickrock
              just barely in bounds

through burnt umber into   fading day terra cotta walls
glint with mica flecks in cliff   shade we fill with seeped dusk
edging near to touch adroit   past scattered ledges aligned
              with asterisms in pooling sky

camp stove flickers   a powdered streak of stars
swallows thoughts on   choosing to be conjoined like river
and canyon or   the secretive leaves of apparently
              bare-stemmed ocotillo

TAKING THE HEAT

now I am molten   blankets thrown back
this winter night to receive   a welcome chill
cool my inner foundry   unseen bellows

at the 4 a.m. waking I picture   lava fields
fire furrows dendrite flows   new channels
what mold can receive this   blossoming heat

    ***

cedar bark tinder   spindle   and board   bow-drill desire
to love and be loved   kitchen hands marked by small
burn scars   I didn't run under the cold tap

I used a smoldering ember once   to sear successively deeper
holes for filbert pecan walnut   a nutting board
to split the shells   without shattering

talk about time   passes   dissolves kisses   disquiet seeps
to temper chocolate   chop   melt over steam
cool   then warm & stir again   to a sheen

    ***

over the edge of the bedclothes   predawn half asleep
down spiral stair   blast of heat   clanging sounds
of a smithy   bring me   my hammer and tongs

FIELD GUISE

Before I walked through the field I saw
a drab, open expanse, hay rounds receding
to dots, scrubby honey-beige swathe a mere

passage to a view of the Blue Ridge.
In the early years I drove by, as worker, lover, wife,
mother, improvised, wove our web each morning—

pick up, drop off, soccer, camping trips, chemo
appointments for their father who died. At the far edge
of vision we once watched a black dog lope past the bales

becoming, visibly, bear. Then they were older. Wet and dry
we walked in the field. Well-worn pocket guides
introduced the neighbors, like the sisters

V. alternifolia and *V. occidentali*s, wingstem and yellow
crownbeard, Verbesinas, from the roots *wer-* to turn,
bend, as sunflowers do, and *werthan*, to become,

as we once named families for their work: Cooper, Smith
Wright, Baker. Wet shoes squish as I lead friends
through goldenrod plumes, naming things.

We're greying—the next disguise. Distinguished now,
the grasses drop all pretense of anonymity; deer tongue
big bluestem, fox sedge, purple lovegrass spread

to the wooded edge, where what look like folded flakes
of bark are buckeye butterflies that flash startled
orange-and-blue wingspots over drainage swales

installed in the 40s by the farmer who plowed this land
before we chose to tend it by letting it alone.
Dogbane and swamp milkweed sidle back.

We find hidden morels at the just-cut verge of the bog,
and amethyst haze over once dull-seeming field—
transcendence in mistflower guise.

IDENTIFYING A SEDGE

Blades rise from ground to arc out
like wild allium, or grocery store leek.
The key wants to know: basal or stem
leaves, or both? We can't tell.
                          These hug
the center, in encircling layers,
then curve away in different
directions, seeking sun. O *Carex*,
impossible to know, caring takes
so many forms. "Sedges have edges,"
to distinguish from grass.
                  We pitch camp
where wild stonecrop and rhododendron
flourish, and synchronous fireflies signal—
their flash-trains a semaphore under
scattered fluff-threatened hemlocks
holding on.
             Edgy, on edge, often,
our love grows concentric—bunched
on a rocky bar that cleaves the stream—
rising stubbornly from river rocks
in dappled shade of rich cove forests.

ANOINTED

frankincense & lavender scent floats
as I focus   time slows
                    you scrub my back   I rub your feet
                          almond oil massage   I run my elbow
            down your spine   locate knots   hollows
stroke with even pressure   symmetry
I sit behind you
                arch your neck up
                    pull to cradle your head   circle temples
            outline jaw   cheekbones   make that butterfly
movement of hands over eyes I learned from you
when it is my turn I sink deeper into my body
                feeling myself from the inside out   with surprise
                    I am I   inhabiting
                bones & sinew   with firm hands you loosen
muscles   stretch & bend me until finally
we nuzzlelick   kiss   rockslip   clasp
            eyes closed   eyes open
                          our crinkles & crow's feet witness
            how ritual makes room   grace notes
spindrift   suffused   fulgent

FIREFLY SEASON

Slowly, warm summer air blurs and chills,
mist seeps in bands above unmown
dogbane, buttonbush, fescue of river field.
Sparkles begin, flashes above grasses, under
saplings, inside dark shrubs, at the crown
and on the ground beneath the black trunk
of the old cottonwood: Chinese lanterns,
called low-slow-glows, early evening fireflies.
This, then is love. Me in rubber boots against
ticks, swatting mosquitoes with the field guide,
your stopwatch timing pulses as Mercury rises.

NOTES

[11]   Epigraph
This quotation is from Rainer Maria Rilke's poem "Buddha in Glory," translated by Stephen Mitchell in *The Selected Poetry of Rainer Maria Rilke*, Bilingual edition, First Vintage, 1984.

[34]   "Stay with Your Guide—Inventor's Studio"
"The witan was the king's council in the Anglo-Saxon government of England from before the seventh century until the eleventh century. It comprised important noblemen, including ealdormen, thegns, and bishops. Meetings of the witan were sometimes called the witenagemot." *Wikipedia*

[53]   "Idiosyncratic Attachments"
The US Federal Energy Regulatory Commission (FERC), is a non-elected body in charge of regulating (some might say promoting) the interstate transmission of electricity, natural gas, and oil. In 2014 Dominion Energy proposed a 600-mile pipeline to move fracked shale gas from the Marcellus shale in Pennsylvania through central Virginia to a series of facilities, including one for export, in Maryland and North Carolina. An unnecessary and redundant pipe, its route targeted rural communities, indigenous and historically Black communities, and ecologically sensitive lands. FERC held the requisite hearings, and members of the public, despite obstacles to access and to the microphone, provided ample comments in protest including the following:

"We have heard that in keeping with Kimball Laundry Co. v. United States (1949), FERC does not concern itself with what was dismissively termed 'landowners' idiosyncratic attachment to their land, but this is at the very heart of our concerns."
—Shannon Farm Association Scoping Meeting Comments, 2015

The author created a series of four outdoor assemblage art and poetry installation trails on threatened lands in the proposed direct path of the pipeline.

[56]   "Entwined"
"The Ties That Bind" is a community-made installation of fabric braids in protest of two fracked-gas pipelines proposed for Virginia. Made initially in protest of the Atlantic Coast Pipeline (ACP), braids were also crafted by citizens threatened by the proposed Mountain Valley Pipeline and displayed at NoMVP protest gatherings and workshops. Although the ACP was cancelled, the MVP is still being litigated.

[60]   "Baked Alaska"
Based on the Alaska Climate Change Strategy Mitigation Advisory Group Executive Summary of the 2009 Final Report. https://dec.alaska.gov/climate-change

[67]   "Inclusion Criteria"
On Monday, June 24, 2019, Oscar Martinez and his daughter Valeria were found drowned along the banks of the Rio Grande. The photograph of the scene by journalist Julia de Luc affected the pubic and lawmakers. https://www.nytimes.com/2019/06/25/us/father-daughter-border-drowning-picture-mexico.html

[74]   "Songs of the Red Velvet Ant"
The red velvet ant is a species of parasitoid wasp native to the eastern United States. The wingless females can deliver a painful sting, earning the nickname "cow killer."

[84]   "Anemone Talks Back"
In dialogue with the poem "Voices About the Princess Anemone" by Stevie Smith, in *Collected Poems*, edited and with a preface by James MacGibbon, 1983, New Directions Books, New York.

photo: Max Johnson

Amelia L. Williams, PhD, a medical writer, hiker, and amateur naturalist, lives in the foothills of the Blue Ridge Mountains. She coordinated "The Ties That Bind: A #NoPipelines Collaborative Art and Story Project" of over 250 fabric braids made by citizens in affected communities to protest proposed fracked-gas pipelines in Virginia. Her full-length poetry collection was a finalist for the 2022 Wandering Aengus Press Book Award. Twice a Pushcart nominee, she served as Assistant Editor with OneEarthSangha and earned a residency at the Hambidge Center. In 2022 she was a semifinalist for the Pablo Neruda Prize for Poetry. Proceeds from her 2016 chapbook, *Walking Wildwood Trail: Poems and Photograph*, benefit local environmental organizations. Her poems and hybrids have appeared in *TAB*, *Streetlight Magazine*, *The Hollins Critic*, *ANMLY*, *Rabbit*, *Nimrod International Journal*, *K'in Literary Journal*, *The Hopper*, *Poetry South*, and elsewhere.

SHANTI ARTS

NATURE • ART • SPIRIT

Please visit us online
to browse our entire book catalog,
including poetry collections and fiction,
books on travel, nature, healing, art,
photography, and more.

Also take a look at our highly regarded art
and literary journal, *Still Point Arts Quarterly*,
which may be downloaded for free.

www.shantiarts.com

www.ingramcontent.com/pod-product-compliance
Lightning Source LLC
Chambersburg PA
CBHW021508090426
42739CB00007B/517